Dear River

poems by

Rachel Sobylya

Finishing Line Press
Georgetown, Kentucky

Dear River

for my mother

Copyright © 2020 by Rachel Sobylya
ISBN 978-1-64662-128-6 First Edition
All rights reserved under International and Pan-American Copyright Conventions. No part of this book may be reproduced in any manner whatsoever without written permission from the publisher, except in the case of brief quotations embodied in critical articles and reviews.

ACKNOWLEDGMENTS

"Loneliness" was first published in issue no. 5 of *West Texas Literary Review* in March of 2018.
"Mountain Dew Mouth" was first published in *Gravel* in March of 2018.
"Boone Lake" was first published in *Likely Red Press* in February of 2019.
"Lenin" was a finalist for the 2018 Rash Award in Poetry and first appeared in *Broad River Review* in 2019.

Special thanks to Caleb Shaw for his help in capturing the cover photograph.

Publisher: Leah Maines
Editor: Christen Kincaid
Cover Art: Caleb Shaw
Author Photo: Maxim Sobylya
Cover Design: Elizabeth Maines McCleavy

Printed in the USA on acid-free paper.
Order online: www.finishinglinepress.com
　　　　　also available on amazon.com

　　　　　　Author inquiries and mail orders:
　　　　　　　　Finishing Line Press
　　　　　　　　　P. O. Box 1626
　　　　　　　Georgetown, Kentucky 40324
　　　　　　　　　　U. S. A.

Table of Contents

Part One: The South
Orangeburg, South Carolina 1
Mountain Dew Mouth 4
Sunday Sermons 5
No Ferry Fee 6
Cardinal 7
Boone Lake 8
Sodom 9
Sensabaugh Tunnel 11
Stranger 12
Geese 13
Sevier County Hot Air Balloon 14
The Holy City 15
Loneliness 16
Reminder 17
Rite 18

Part Two: Everywhere Else
Confession 20
Sochi 21
Neva River 22
Lenin 23
Suburb: 4:00 AM 24
Forecasted Rain 25
The Other Man 26
Drawl 27
Sophomore English 28
The Memory Room 29
Reconciliation 30
Immutability 32
Autumn 33
Dear River 34

Part One: The South

Orangeburg, South Carolina
for my grandmother

has the finest pecans in the world,
the blackest river I've ever seen,
more pines than a Tennessee Christmas card,
and my mother's history.

If I close my eyes, I can smell the needles,
remember stepping out of an '88 Cadillac Brougham,
feet sinking slightly in the gritty driveway,
Southern sand soil.

But, more than this memory, I think of the story I cannot forget.
I think of the girl my mother saw drown in the pond,
five miles out from the homeplace,
tangled in the twisted, grappling roots beneath peaceful water lilies.

Then, I can see the garden the way it was,
my grandmother bent at the waist
tending tomatoes, my grandfather at work
in the tool shed beneath the pear tree.

His sons there with him too, once,
so I imagined 'cause they were all gone,
scattered across the state and memory
by the time I got there.

All except an uncle,
but he's gone now, too,
like my grandfather, who lingers
only in the scent of fresh pears.

I remember the folklore spat
in the trailer's living room
with a tin roof, a few rooms
tacked on over the years.

Car wrecks, camp outs, church picnics.
I could convince myself I was there,
with younger versions of my mother's family.
Three of these characters are dead now.

Orangeburg, South Carolina
has the dustiest dirt roads.
I remember getting lost on one with cousins,
where the humidity seeped into our bones and back out our skin.

Blackberry bushes full of thorns, copperheads
camouflaged as thin branches
skimming the surface of the Edisto River
below the Spanish moss

hanging low, tickling the water, tempting,
like the inviting willow tree two miles
from that gritty driveway, but hiding ghosts
from hangings: sins of the South.

The plinking of summer rain
especially on the back porch,
where cigarettes and sweet tea
were offered in abundance.

Morning glories bloomed like clockwork
and Carolina anoles scampered away
from my cousins' fingers,
leaving writhing tails behind.

Though none could've predicted
such an ill-omened future.
Only one uncle is left there,
lonely beneath his stone at the First Baptist Church.

No one has been to that blue trailer,
garden deer have gnawed down,
decaying tool shed
in a long while.

Generations, memory, history
left to rot, while we try to sell
that plot of land in
Orangeburg, South Carolina.

Mountain Dew Mouth

exists above South Carolina,
below Pennsylvania,
in the mountains
where coal miners dig brown land
for black rocks;
rotting smiles,
open mouths rimmed with dirt, house
tiny tree stumps with scattered spaces
in two, jagged rows,
asymmetrical like the rows of forest
laid down by timber barons in the 1900's.
Diseased, broken pearls covered in spittle,
darkened by tobacco pouches
pushing bottom lips forward,
enamel defeated by the contents of cans
imprinted on back pockets
in Appalachian hollers,
welcome the green, carbonated liquid
determined to fester in Appalachian incisors.

Sunday Sermons

I bleed coins into pooled blood, which is really
a red circle of felt lining the bottom of a golden offertory plate
passed from one unholy hand to the next.
Coins hard earned from weekly chores.
Coins I *should* tithe.
God told the bible, the bible told Mom, Mom told me.

It's hot, even the stained glass sweats
along with us sinners perched in the pews
like ravens receiving manna from our preacher.
Condensation drips down Mary's stained glass face to my right,
and my sister's to my left.

My shoulder touches my brother's.
We're crammed in tight this morning.
Pastor Wayne preaches on Revelations, but
I'm distracted by red hymnals, half, eraser-less pencils,
and the tic-tac-toe game my brother and I play
in the margins of our bibles
between glances at Mom, hoping she doesn't notice.

One time, my brother told me kids pee in the baptismal.
Pastor Wayne doesn't say anything, but he must know.
The water must get a little less clear, but still clean enough to wash
sins away. I try not to laugh while I listen to Pastor Wayne's sermon,
but I can't help imagining him standing in a baptismal full of shame.

No Ferry Fee

A blacksnake
slithers along the
curved sides of a canoe.
Imprisoned and unknowingly
awaiting the guillotine.
My brother delivers
a quick blow.
It enters the afterlife
blind, deaf, mute,
head separated from heart,
without two pennies for the boatman.

Cardinal

One November evening the stray cat
that frequents our back door delivered a gift:
a broken cardinal,
a distorted, dragged along body,
hanging from its jaws.

It lay still, waited for the last
cut of claw, few violent paw shakes
that would rid its hooked, feather thin bones
from the paw that ensnared them.
Its wing was strung out like a red laundry line,

mimicking the motion of flight,
as if there could be a last attempt,
one final, flirting swoop, close call,
escape at the last moment,
a playful torment repeated hundreds of times.

But the Lord seeks penance for pride,
and the feline devil dared deliver it.
My heart ached for the poor bird,
timid in its humility, absorbed in a natural cruelty
I hoped it understood.

All there knew the bird would never fly again—
the cat, leisurely outstretched with its catch
on its curved claw, the bird, unmoving
save tiny gasps, and myself, wondering
if all sins must be paid.

There was no blood, no final convulsion,
and the cat sauntered off, eventually.
The bird simply looked toward the dimming sky,
light polluted stars, barely visible waning moon,
as it waited for a death shroud of fresh snow.

Boone Lake

Moonlight glints off mason jars
huddled 'round our feet in the bottom of the canoe
squished together with flashlights, fishing poles.

Our oars break the picture of stars
with each smooth stroke
propelling us across the lake.

We paddle wide past the dam
eluding the turbine whirlpools
catching cautionless fish,

as water spills over concrete shoots.
We steer close to shores avoiding
marine police and late night motor boaters.

Sticking our oars straight down
we still the boat, relinquish ourselves
to the depths of the lake. We bait hooks,

cast them far away from uncapped moonshine,
denim shorts, bare feet relieved of flip flops
rocking with each uneven wave in the shadows of mountains.

We imagine bull bluegill,
age-less, big bellied catfish tempted
by the baited, curved hooks bobbing in the dark water.

Our palms bat mosquitoes,
folding every now and again, to cup water
splashing it across our humid heated faces.

We don't catch anything,
except a buzz and one scare
from a string of lights on a nearby dock

flashing red, blue for a split second
or so it seemed
on the tail end of a broken gaze.

Sodom
    New Orleans, LA

I

Wicked voodoo caricatures smile
from shop windows.
Guises for masquerades
framing displays, enticing tourists

with Old World iron wrought balconies
line second stories of buildings
selling hurricanes, gumbo
to thirsty, hungry tourists

stampede Café du Monde
for authentic beignets,
creole cafes serving
jambalaya, crawfish étouffée

and views of ferry boats
tethered alongside barges
boasting cargo of all kinds
dumped at the mouth

of the Mississippi River,
the Gulf of Mexico
that swallowed up the town
in 2005.

II

I was in the tenth grade.
We had to write about Katrina,
about what happened,
for my sophomore English class,

but what did we know of such things?

I only remembered our brief visit,
my father's words:
It's a modern day Sodom,
and how much I loved it anyway.

The cacophony of jazz chords
overlapping each other,
Jackson Square humming
with bustling people

not stopping to watch the artist
skewing chalk lines, blending
them into art. But I watched him
watch my sister, wink at her, and laugh.

Sensabaugh Tunnel

Once we drank much, got bored, decided to go
to Sensabaugh Tunnel in Kingsport.
We took turns passing around Black & Milds
during the thirty minute ride to the next town over.

The story goes that Ed Sensabaugh went mad one night
in 1920, probably from too much jake leg moonshine,
and killed his wife, children, even their newborn baby.
He tossed their bodies in an old, damp tunnel.

The city paved it in the 70's, but *they* say
if you turn off your car, roll your windows down,
you'll hear his labored footsteps, a baby's whine,
and your car'll never start up again.

I was scared shitless by the time we took the exit,
and my friends teased, encouraging a few more swigs
from a flask they passed to the back seat. When we arrived
we dawdled around, too proud to admit fear.

It was 2:00 am, and left over rain still splattered
bits of the windshield. Our driver rolled in
the tunnel, down the windows. It was damp and pitch black.
She killed the lights, engine. We waited.

But we didn't hear a baby's cry, heavy footsteps.
It was chilly from the night air, stank of mildew,
and I was more afraid another car would drive through
the other side and hit us head on in the darkness of the tunnel.

Stranger

This is how I'll always remember Daddy.
My aunt passed me a photo
of my grandfather, one out of the fifty
or so scattered about our crossed legs
being sorted, picked through in an attempt to find ten
perfect pictures to capsulate his life.

There was my grandfather in his prime,
after a war, before the death of his son.
I stared hard at him
staring at me through the glossy print
almost crossing the impossible forty year gap in time.

His tattoos were bright,
every color, curve unspoiled by age spots.
They no longer resembled bruised fruit.
His hair jet black, like my mother's,
not the snowy down I'll forever remember.
His eyes stern, long before age softened their harshness.

He stood at the trailer's kitchen sink
holding a glass of orange juice
so far away from the man
who couldn't leave South Carolina
who was about to be buried in Tennessee.

Geese

Geese mate for life. Did you know that?

She knew
because one day two geese flew onto their land
and stayed and lived and died.

We named them Gerdy and Gertrude.
Wherever one went, the other followed.

I looked at my mother's face,
creases deepening as she pulled
memory forward,
and I wondered how many *geese*
flew in and out of her life.

We came home from school one day,
and one of them was dead.
Soon after, the other left too.
We figured it'd just gone off to die.

Sevier County Hot Air Balloon Festival

They float above us,
like swollen bellies,
as if full of the hot breaths
we exude below them.
All our words bubbled up
in an elastic explosion
of patterned mayhem,
chaos from below organized,
somehow suspended,
in an inescapable nonsense.
We can't tear our eyes from
the absurdity of the
welcomed distraction
waiting to bear our burdens,
float them away,
for a day.

The Holy City
      Charleston, SC

has 400 churches within its limits,
and all are filled with congregations
come Sunday morning
because that's how it's been
for over 300 years.

We're on a walking tour;
the guide rambles off facts.
Crepe myrtles growing
since the Civil War line streets;
their pink and purple flowered vines reach out
from trunks in light breezes.

I don't know this tour was worth $20/person.
My feet are killing me,
and my family is lagging behind the group
because my brother is joking
that an old pay phone in Battery Park
is the most ancient artifact we've seen yet.

The guide tells us of ghosts that roam
docks at the port, dangle from trees in yards.
He mentions the Cravens, our namesake,
a founding family. We aren't proud.
Most tourists now don't remember how unholy
this holy city once was,

how God punished this city by the sea,
after the war,
and set his people free.

Loneliness

Here we are alone,
waiting on the inevitable
to reach down and push us
together, away from the ones
waiting for us, tending our children.

Toeing the line,
we are already drowning
in the lake of stars above us,
and the moon is a sickle
waiting to slice down with morning.

Reminder

I spilled the bottle
of perfume:
your last reminder.

It was half full,
and tiny shards spewed
away from the fall
like pieces of lost memory.

An explosion of you
overwhelmed, and
even after mopping you linger
strong as you did in life.

Each time I sweep the spot
you stained, broom bristles release you
and flood me
when I'm close to them

sweeping debris into the pan.

Rite

I. Pilgrimage

It was early summer,
when dew stays in droplets
beyond the sunrise, and the cool of night
lingers in early morning.

We crossed the state line
into North Carolina,
which felt like Tennessee,
just as still, only a little cooler.

Our tires roamed from asphalt
to gritty gravel, to a dirty road,
sticky and rust colored from a recent rain,
to a full stop in front of a rural descent

leading deep into the belly of the mountain.
We stepped out, stretched sedated limbs;
then you offered your hand
as we stumbled our way down

to meet the stagnant pools cut off from the river vein,
joined in a meager marriage by miniscule capillaries
slowly cutting through ancient sedimentary slabs.
I hoped one day the mini vessels might meet the river,

manage to meander their splitting ways
down deep and far wide, but if they could at all,
it would be long after me and you
and the world might be raptured by then, anyway.

We trekked the miniature moss lands
growing on each shelf of every slab
slick at the touch. You helped me there,
over jutting rocks, through ankle deep water.

The torrents rushed through the woods
toward our ears, and eventually flooded our vision
with the mighty pool receiving the rage
of the mouth of the mountain, which could've been God's,

ready to swallow us up, hold us down
with aquatic ropes until our redemption,
and I feared facing a fate like the boy
who drowned here two years ago.

II. Baptism

Only the rapture exists
at the bottom of a waterfall, a vacant second coming
that welcomes you only
with a greeting from the dead, which is why

I think I feel the drowned boy
brush against my leg while I wait
for buoyance, deaf and blind and cold and numb,
as an endowment of understanding is bestowed:

> Mr. Sayer's lesson on vacuums,
> void of everything, full of nothing.
> Pastor Wayne's sermon on submergence
> in holy water for cleansing and rebirth—
> a marriage of evolution, revelation, of known, unknown.

I find what I'd sought, I think,
and there was no boatman after all,
so I surface, gulping air, panting, seeing
you sitting on a rock and waving

because you were too scared to jump
and unaware of the revival below.

Part Two: Everywhere Else

Confession

My mother has much aged,
and each time I see her,
twice a year on holidays,
I am aghast.

We are similar in visage,
yet I have stolen
her youthful face.

I lie when she asks
if she looks old
because I am afraid
to tell the truth,
frightened to lose her former face,
ashamed the new one will wedge itself
too tightly in my memories

as a reminder of time,
and how my own rites of passage passed.
Clock clicks tick off milestones in my own life,
and leave small traces
at the top of my forehead,
corners of my eyes.

I am afraid even now
as I pen this confession.

Sochi

We stay in your aunt's room,
selflessly given to welcome back
a prodigal nephew and American bride.
We listen to the city sounds,
like the tinkering of small minds
whispering inventions to themselves.
We watch the divider curtain
relinquish herself to soft wind's will.
We sleep atop covers
feeling humidity rising from the sea below.
We drink coffee, the American way,
made for me, the new daughter,
and taste bitter grinds at cup bottoms.

Here is where you were,
always, before me,
listening to city bustle,
watching this curtain,
feeling hot humidity,
drinking tea instead of coffee.

Neva River

The wind slices deeply,
the spray from the river
mists our faces with a new chill,
and my focus for the few words
I might recognize tries to smother the cold.
Focus and your low voice whispering English,
your accent thick since returning
to St. Petersburg, after Moscow, before Sochi.
The smushed together buildings blur,
though I try to remember them all—
the castle Rasputin fled from,
the breaking of the horses at each corner of the bridge,
a landing on which Dostoyevsky stepped,
but it's bitter cold in July,
as I always suspected it would be.

Lenin

Early morning, Moscow rain in July,
and we huddle for warmth as we wait in line.
Back in Tennessee, my high school history teacher told us
the Communist was encased in a mausoleum,
the revolutionary eternally unburied.

I was a long way from my high school self,
married to a Russian man,
standing with my Russian family,
listening to their mutterings of decision making,
catching bits of words, pieces of sound
that hold no meaning for me.

We enter, sheltered from the rain, finally.
The guards shush the elderly lady ahead of us
as we shuffle down the dim hallway, small set of stairs,
until we arrive at his resting room.

The harsh light above yellows his sallow cheeks,
glistens his forehead, shadows his goatee.
His fingers curl into each other,
gentle fists, as if ready to rise
again, to remind of the first redemption,
eternally, fitfully resting in wait.

Suburb: 4:00 AM

I let the dog out,
coo encouragement
at her as the humidity sneaks
into the crooks of my crossed elbows,
creeps down my sternum,
slips past the center of my chest.

It is too light to see stars,
not for lack of darkness
but for the illumination of street lights
paid for by my taxes or HOA fees or both or neither.

But the dog is done before I think further
or slip into dwelling on the last time
I saw clear stars, which is masked
by all the times I haven't.

Forecasted Rain

At a distance
it is a half pulled drape,
and sunlight peeks
between soft folds.

Then, it's loosed,
gathering all in a shroud,
sweepingly replenishing
with mercy, drying up the thirst

'cause we needed it here,
and we watched for its coming
among the sunlight
across the prairie.

The Other Man

He stands there teeming with possibility.
It rises alongside his angled face
and down deep dimples.
It seeps from each emphatic eyebrow raise
and beckons at the corner of his mouth
before settling on charismatically crooked teeth.

My own lover stands at the other end of the bar,
broad and highbrowed with familiarity
etched thin into sleepy eyelids.
It slides down his askew nose,
gives freely from flushed cheeks,
and pools on the edge of his smile.

Familiarity so known to me that I hardly notice
possibility in his own deep dimples,
emphatic eyebrow raises,
charismatically crooked teeth.

Drawl

You've been visiting in my dreams,
and I love you as much as I did then.
I remember everything you say,
but I cannot hear the sound of your voice,
cannot pinpoint its pitches,
long drawls I know must still exist,
sweet like syrup sifted through a sieve,
tiny sounds of breath lingering
in long, Virginian vowels.
I cannot hear the "I love you"
that came too late and only in writing
anyway, you always sounded sleepy,
which is why I dream of you at night.

Sophomore English

For my student in the second desk in the third row
please stop begging for forgiveness for asking questions.
I have so many too, but I no longer ask them.

The Memory Room

is really a small storage closet
in our spare bedroom,
but I go there sometimes
to dig through boxes and remember
all the things I've forgotten:
the photo of my childhood dog
cut into a heart,
a 100% in bright red
on a 4th grade spelling test,
my grandfather's obituary
bluntly brief,
the letters we wrote each other,
hoping to write away the gaps,
my homecoming queen tiara,
slightly bent on one side,
a wedding program,
printed on silver shimmered paper.

Mostly I go there
after a glass of wine,
hoping to find
what was never lost.

Reconciliation

There is a tight chord
wrung round my memory
ready to be strung into meaning,

and the first note is a long road
with one blue house, a garden,
and a basket of pears on a washing machine
near spoiled from the heat of
the Southern Carolina.

But the second note is sick,
an immediate shift of association
with the past, a past some talk about
and some don't talk about
and some talk about but in the wrong way.

The sins of my ancestors,
the houses with hanging front doors,
desolate yards, and schools still segregated
all because of my *kind*.

Yet the third note is a patriarch
piddling with the engine of a '79 Ford,
a matriarch with huge rimmed glasses
watering Morning Glories at a window.

This sound is a love so deep
it cannot be silenced,
an incorruptible thing
steeped in nostalgia and childhood idealism.

How do I reconcile these notes into harmony?
What is the probability of peace
between such sustained turmoil
since the beginning of our history?

This terrible melody has been played
during American offertories
in hot churches for centuries.
Here is all I offer:

The South is a symphony,
a sad, low churning
against all that's past
and all that will come to pass,
each instrument of memory crying out for
recognition, recompense, and recovery.

Immutability

Appalachia runs deep in me.
Its striations stripe my blood,
like the colored lines
on mountain interiors—
the ones you see when driving
through dynamited centers
on curvy North Carolina parkways.

It runs in long lines,
mixing in veins,
twisting, rooting through each crevice,
touching every organ,
filling every sense.

It lies there quietly,
a chronic pain waiting to flair
when a near forgotten familiar accent speaks,
a television program spans a mountain range,
I read the poem about the red fox at Christmas
again.

Autumn

When the wheat tips bellow in the wind
does the whisper reach you,
slide its fingers near your ear
tell you of the harvest, fruitful,
the gathering to be done, quickly,
and without you?

Do you miss it then?
Confess your devil deal,
fair trade-
wheat fields, unfenced,
for a concrete slab, fenced,
stars, clear as cold mornings,
for streetlights, dim as humidity
at mid day.

Dear River,

Do you ever think of me
        when the world is too still?

Do you remember my hands
        running over your rocky breasts?

Can you feel my oar
        split your soft skin?

Can you see me kissing others
        on the edge of your sandy bank?

Do you imagine me
        lapped up in your mouth?

Do you not know
        how much I think of you?

Here in this humid hole
where you can't justify jealousy
because there are no others.

Rachel Sobylya grew up in Johnson City, TN, and holds a B.A. in English and a B.A. in History from East Tennessee State University. She has always loved writing, but it wasn't until her time as a graduate student at Dartmouth College that she began to write consistently. Being away from her hometown allowed her insight into the regions that shaped her life: Appalachia and the South, and her writing is inspired by her eccentric extended family, three younger siblings, Appalachia's mountains and landscape, and her mother. Although writing is her first love, Rachel is also passionate about teaching. She was a teaching assistant as a graduate student, and she began teaching at Pellissippi State Community College in Knoxville, TN after graduating from Dartmouth. Although she didn't originally see herself as a teacher while she was in college, she has found it is her calling. She currently teaches high school English in Katy, TX and adjuncts with Houston Community College. This is her first chapbook of poetry.

www.ingramcontent.com/pod-product-compliance
Lightning Source LLC
LaVergne TN
LVHW041600070426
835507LV00011B/1210